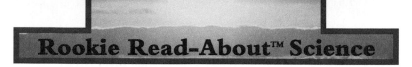

It Could Still Be A Rock

By Allan Fowler

Consultants:
Robert L. Hillerich, Ph.D., Bowling Green
State University, Bowling Green, Ohio

Mary Nalbandian, Director of Science,
Chicago Public Schools, Chicago, Illinois

Fay Robinson, Child Development Specialist

CHILDRENS PRESS®
CHICAGO

Design by Beth Herman Design Associates

Library of Congress Cataloging–in–Publication Data

Fowler, Allan

    It could still be a rock / by Allan Fowler.

      p. cm. –(Rookie read-about science)

    Includes index.

    Summary: Discusses the size, shape, composition, origin and other
aspects of different kinds of rocks.

    ISBN 0-516-06010-4

    1. Rocks–Juvenile literature. [1. Rocks.] I. Title.

  II. Series: Fowler, Allan. Rookie read-about science.

QE432.2.F69 1993

552–dc20   92-39260

                                            CIP

                                           AC

A rock could be any size and still be a rock.

It could be a grain of sand,
a tiny pebble, a little stone,
or a large boulder.

It could be the size
of a mountain like the
Rock of Gibraltar.

Or it could be as big as the whole Earth – because the Earth is made of rock.

So is the Moon.

This rock is a piece of
the Moon, brought back
by astronauts.

Granite and marble are
very hard rocks. Many
big buildings are made
of granite and marble.

But the marbles you play
with aren't made of
marble. They're usually
made of glass.

Rock could be red-hot and flowing, and still be rock.

Lava is the melted rock
that flows out of a volcano.

There's even a rock you can set on fire. People once used this rock to cook their food and heat their homes.

You know this rock – it's coal.

15

But did you know that all the coal in the world used to be plants?

These rocks used to be trees, but they are rock today. We say that the trees became petrified.

17

Yes, living things can
change into rocks.

But it takes a very long
time – millions of years.

Fossils are the remains of plants or animals that are found in rock.

They show us what living
things looked like, even
though they lived millions
of years ago.

How did the plants or
animals get inside rock?

When they died, their
bodies were covered
by mud, clay, or other
materials.

As ages went by, the layers
of material around the
plant or animal hardened
into rock.

Some rocks, like this limestone, were formed at the bottom of the sea.

Seas once covered many
places that are dry land now.

Everything changes
in time.

Wind and water wear
rocks away slowly –
very slowly – and change
the shapes of rocks.

27

So something might be
shaped like a bridge,
or a table – and it could
still be a rock

It might even have a
fish inside it – and still
be a rock.

Words You Know

rocks

pebbles

stones

boulder

Earth

Moon

limestone

granite

marble

Rock of Gibraltar

coal

lava

petrified

fossil

Index

About the Author

Allan Fowler is a free-lance writer with a background in advertising. Born in New York, he lives in Chicago now and enjoys traveling.

Photo Credits

Field Museum of Natural History #CK5T, Chicago – 18-19

Field Museum of Natural History #GEO84989c, Chicago – 29

NASA – 7, 9, 30 (center left)

PhotoEdit – ©John Neubauer, 10, 30 (bottom right); ©David Young-Wolff, 20, 31 (bottom right); ©Elena Rooraid, 23

Photri – 13

SuperStock International, Inc. – ©William Hamilton, 5, 31 (top); ©Gary Louzon, 8, 30 (center right); ©Roger Allyn Lee, 11; ©Manley, 17, 31 (bottom left); ©Tom Algire, 25; ©Steve Vidler, 28; ©Mark Keller, 30 (top left); ©Leonard Lee Rue, 30 (top right)

Valan – ©Chris Malazdrewicz, 4; ©V. Wilkinson, 15, 31 (center left); ©J.E. Stevenson, 15 (inset); ©John Cancalosi, 21; ©Tom W. Parkin, 24, 30 (bottom left); ©Deborah Vanslet, 30 (bottom center)

Visuals Unlimited – ©John Gerlach, Cover, 27; ©D. Cavagnaro, 12, 31 (center right); ©Valerie Hodgson, 30 (top center)

COVER: Delicate Arch, Utah

3